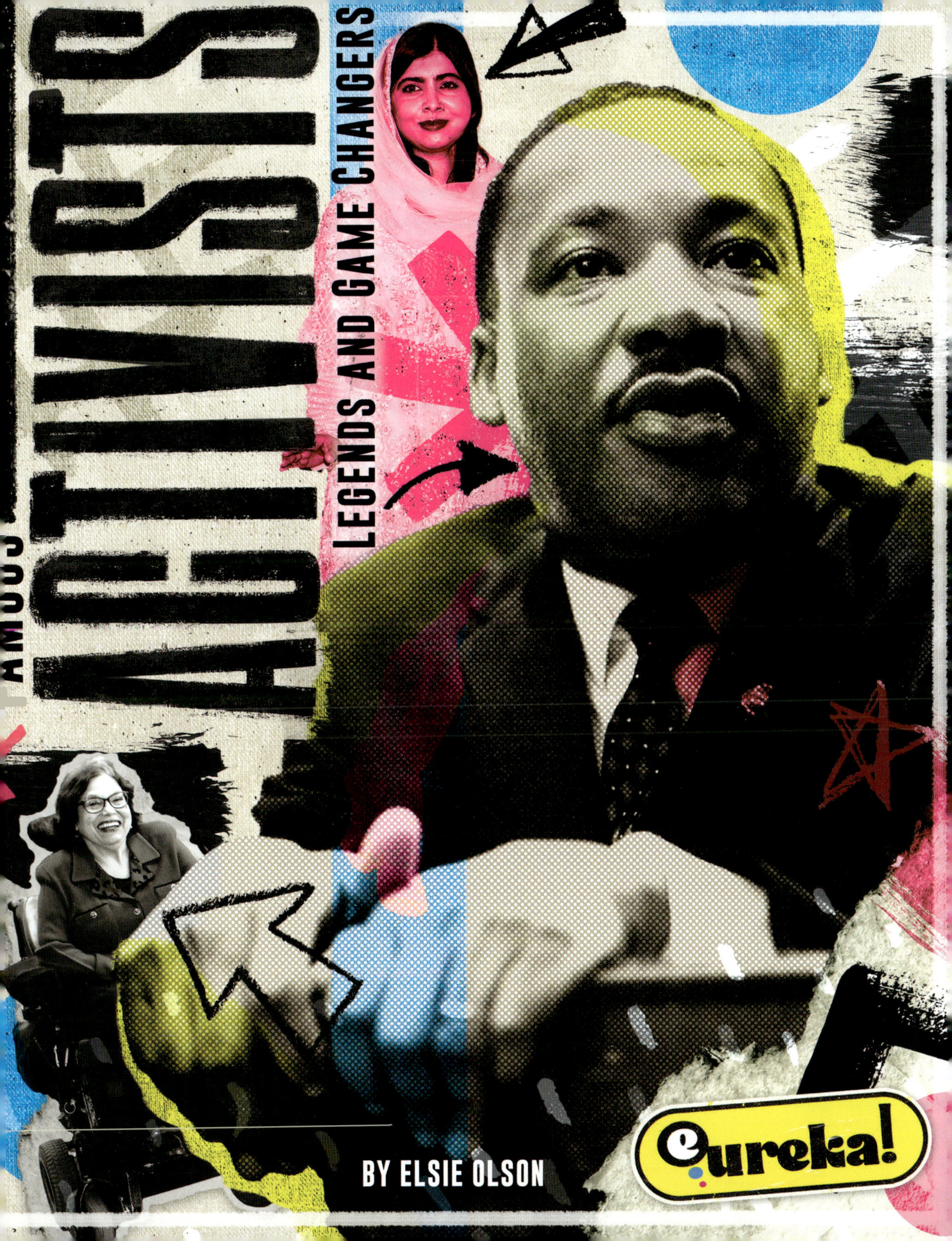

FAMOUS ACTIVISTS

LEGENDS AND GAME CHANGERS

BY ELSIE OLSON

eureka!

Eureka! books turn real stories into unforgettable experiences. This nonfiction imprint sparks curiosity, encourages critical thinking, and engages middle-grade readers. *Eureka!* books empower young minds to explore the stories of the real world, one fascinating fact at a time. Unravel the power of knowledge and lifelong learning with *Eureka!*

This edition first published in 2026 by Bellwether Media, Inc.

Library of Congress Cataloging-in-Publication Data

LC record for Famous Activists available at: https://lccn.loc.gov/2025020035

Editor: Betsy Rathburn   Designer: Jeffrey Kollock

Printed in the United States of America, North Mankato, MN.

TABLE OF CONTENTS

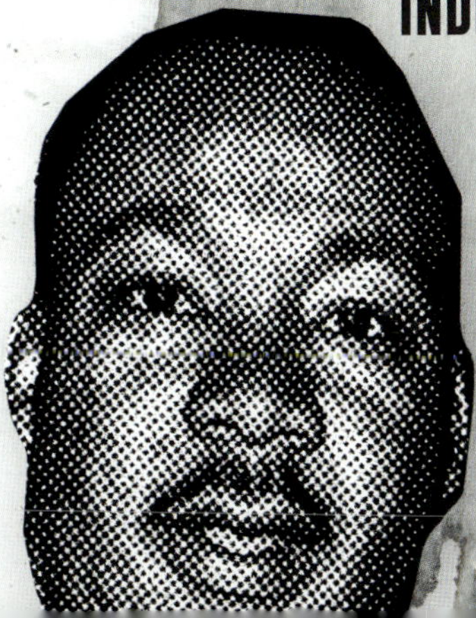

ACTIVISM HISTORY

Activists are people who fight for certain causes. Some fight for human rights or civil rights. Others demand fair treatment for animals. Still others work toward protecting the environment. Anything that people believe in is something that activists may fight for.

There are many ways to do activism. Protests are a common form of activism. People gather in public places to demand change from leaders. They may make signs, chant slogans, and give speeches. Marches are similar. People walk a certain route to bring attention to their cause. Boycotts are another common form of activism. People stop buying a certain product or visiting a certain place. This pressures the owner to change. Strikes are when workers stop working until their employer meets certain demands.

Activism can also be done behind the scenes. People who write letters to leaders or post about their causes on social media are acting as activists. Mutual aid is giving money to help better the local community. It is a form of activism, too. When activists come together, they can change the world!

TIMELINE

1635 Ireland passes the first known farm animal welfare law

1833 the United Kingdom passes the Factory Act of 1833 to support better conditions for factory workers

1865 the 13th Amendment outlaws slavery in the U.S.

1920 the 19th Amendment gives women in the U.S. the right to vote

1945 the UN forms in part to protect human rights around the world

1955–1956 a bus boycott in Montgomery, Alabama, becomes a defining moment of the U.S. civil rights movement

1972 Title IX bans gender-based discrimination in U.S. schools

1973 the U.S. passes the Endangered Species Act to protect animals at risk of extinction

1990 the Americans with Disabilities Act is the world's first law written to protect people with disabilities

2015 same-sex marriage is legalized in all U.S. states

2015 196 countries agree to take steps to prevent climate change in the Paris Agreement

ENVIRONMENTAL ACTIVISM

In the 1960s, many people became concerned about how human activity affected the air and water. In 1970, U.S. senator Gaylord Nelson established Earth Day. It helped raise awareness for environmental issues. Today, many environmental activists fight to lessen the impact of **climate change**.

CIVIL RIGHTS ACTIVISM

Civil rights are individual rights guaranteed by a government regardless of race, religion, gender, or ability. They include the right to vote and the right to a fair trial. In the 1950s and 1960s, members of the U.S. civil rights movement fought for equal rights for Black Americans.

HUMAN RIGHTS ACTIVISM

Human rights are the rights of every human, no matter where they live or what their background is. These include freedom from violence, access to a fair trial, and freedom of religion. Activists worldwide work to protect human rights.

MORE ACTIVISM, MORE ACTIVISTS!

ANIMAL RIGHTS ACTIVISM

Animal rights activists work to make sure animals are treated fairly. In 1954, the Humane Society of the United States formed to fight for animal welfare. Today, much of animal activism focuses on the treatment of farm animals and ending animal testing.

NELSON MANDELA

Nelson Mandela was a South African activist. He worked against **apartheid**. He spent almost 30 years in prison for his actions. In 1990, he was released. He went on to become South Africa's first Black president. He is remembered for helping end apartheid.

WINONA LADUKE

Winona LaDuke fights for the rights of Native Americans. She leads protests, gives speeches, and writes books. She advocates for **Indigenous** peoples' rights to their land, cultural practices, and natural resources.

TARANA BURKE

From a young age, Tarana Burke advocated for others. She led projects focused on housing, racism, and more. In 2006, she started the #MeToo movement. It grew rapidly in 2017 as attention around violence and abuse against women grew.

MAHATMA GANDHI

Mahatma Gandhi was an Indian activist who opposed violence. He led the movement for India's independence from Great Britain using nonviolent resistance. This included boycotting British goods and protesting the British government.

ENVIRONMENTAL ACTIVISTS

When Greta Thunberg was 15 years old, she began a weekly climate strike. Soon, young people around the world were protesting just like her. The protests made Thunberg an icon for environmental activists.

Greta Thunberg

GETTING HER START

As a child, Thunberg saw a video about climate change. She decided to do something to help. She convinced her family to stop using animal products and flying in airplanes. Her parents installed solar panels on their home. But Thunberg wanted to do more.

FRIDAYS FOR FUTURE

In 2018, Thunberg began skipping school each Friday to protest outside of the Swedish parliament. She held a sign that read *Skolstrejk för Klimatet*, or "School Strike for Climate." She hoped to raise awareness about climate change and pressure politicians to do something. Her protests became the Fridays for Future movement.

THE GRETA EFFECT

In 2019, Thunberg gave a famous speech at a United Nations (UN) event. She scolded world leaders for caring more about money than about climate change. Many people were inspired by her! People began calling her influence "the Greta effect."

THE WORK CONTINUES

Thunberg continues to speak out about climate change. She gives speeches around the world. She also organizes and attends protests. She has become one of the loudest voices in the environmental movement!

BORN: January 3, 2003, in Stockholm, Sweden

EDUCATION: Franska Skolan, a private secondary school in Stockholm

KNOWN FOR: raised awareness for climate change

AWARDS AND HONORS

- **2019** Rachel Carson Prize
- **2019** International Children's Peace Prize
- **2020** Gulbenkian Prize for Humanity

SUPERPOWER

Thunberg has autism spectrum disorder (ASD). This affects how she interacts with others. She has described it as her superpower.

TIMELINE

2018 begins her Fridays for Future climate strikes

2019 addresses the UN in New York City

2021 helps organize a series of concerts called Climate Live to bring attention to climate change

2023 finishes high school and ends her Friday climate strikes

In 2019, 14-year-old Autumn Peltier was named the Anishinabek Nation's Chief Water Commissioner. Her job was to make sure her people had access to safe drinking water. Peltier's activism has earned her the nickname "Water Warrior."

Autumn Peltier

INSPIRED TO ACT

Peltier grew up on Canada's Manitoulin Island in Lake Huron. When she was 8 years old, she traveled to a nearby First Nations community. Signs said the water was not safe to drink. Peltier learned that many First Nations communities did not have access to clean water. She looked for ways to help.

MEETING THE PRIME MINISTER

In 2016, Peltier met Canadian prime minister Justin Trudeau. She told him she was upset with him for not protecting Canada's water. A video of Peltier talking to Trudeau went viral. It drew attention to First Nations' struggles for clean water.

FAMILY ACTIVISM

Peltier was inspired to take action by her great aunt, Josephine Mandamin. Mandamin was a famous water activist who walked around the Great Lakes to draw attention to the Indigenous water crisis.

TIMELINE

2016 meets Canadian Prime Minister Justin Trudeau

2018 gives a speech to the UN General Assembly

WARRIOR UP!

In 2018, Peltier gave a speech to representatives of 193 nations of the UN, telling the leaders to "warrior up." She encouraged them to do more to protect water sources. Three years later, Peltier launched a **petition** demanding clean water for Indigenous peoples. It received more than 100,000 signatures.

THE FIGHT CONTINUES

Peltier continues to fight for clean water. In 2023, she also began studying crime at the University of Ottawa. In the future, she hopes to help Indigenous people affected by crime.

AWARDS AND HONORS

- **2018** Ottawa Riverkeeper Award
- **2022** Ontario Human Rights Commission Daniel G. Hill Award
- **2023** Canada Walk of Fame Community Hero Award

BORN: September 27, 2004, on Manitoulin Island, Ontario, Canada

EDUCATION: University of Ottawa

KNOWN FOR: fought for Indigenous access to clean water

2019 is named Chief Water Commissioner for the Anishinabek Nation

2021 launches a petition to the Canadian government demanding clean water

2023 begins studying crime at the University of Ottawa

Rachel Carson

Rachel Carson was a scientist and writer. Her work changed the way many people thought about nature. It encouraged lawmakers to pass new laws protecting the environment.

TIMELINE

1936 begins working at what is now the U.S. Fish and Wildlife Service

1941 publishes her first book, *Under the Sea-Wind*

1952 wins the National Book Award for nonfiction for *The Sea Around Us*

1955 publishes *The Edge of the Sea*

1962 publishes *Silent Spring*

A LOVE OF NATURE

Carson loved nature as a child. She also loved writing. She went to college to study English. But she changed her mind and graduated with a degree in biology. Eventually, she found work with what is now the U.S. Fish and Wildlife Service. She taught about biology in radio programs. She also wrote for magazines and newspapers.

WATER WRITER

In 1941, Carson published her first book, *Under the Sea-Wind*. It was about the ocean. Two more books about the ocean followed. One book, *The Sea Around Us*, won the National Book Award in 1952. Carson was now a famous author and scientist.

AWARDS AND HONORS

- **1952** National Book Award
- **1963** Audubon Medal
- **1980** Presidential Medal of Freedom

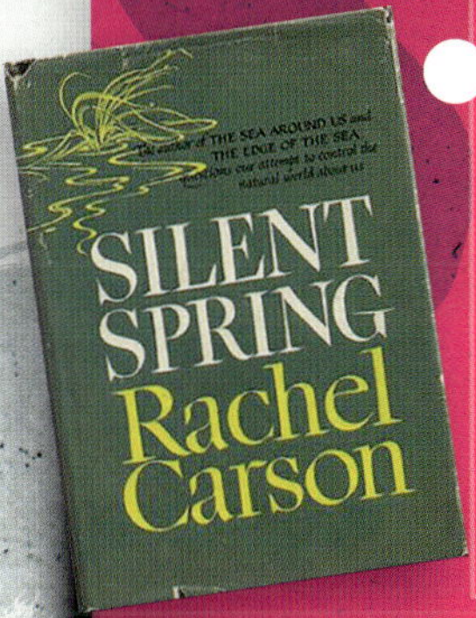

SILENT SPRING

By the 1950s, Carson had become concerned about the impact of **pesticides** on animal life. This led her to research the chemicals. She realized pesticides such as DDT were harming the environment. Her research led to the 1962 book *Silent Spring*. Many, including some chemical companies, were angry about her findings. Still, the book changed the way many people felt about pesticides.

INSPIRING THE FUTURE

Carson died in 1964. But her legacy continues. In 1972, the U.S. banned the use of DDT. In 2004, DDT was banned for most uses worldwide.

> "The history of life on earth has been a history of interaction between living things and their surroundings."
> — Rachel Carson, *Silent Spring*

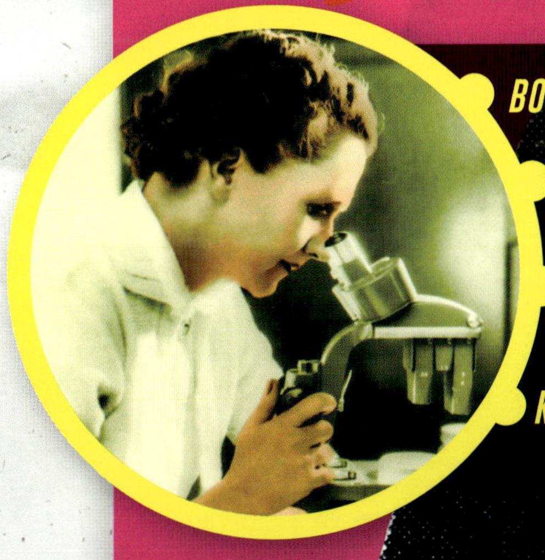

BORN: May 27, 1907, in Springdale, Pennsylvania

DIED: April 14, 1964

EDUCATION: Pennsylvania College for Women, Johns Hopkins University, Marine Biological Laboratory

KNOWN FOR: wrote *Silent Spring* and helped stop the use of DDT

Jerome Foster II is a leader in the youth climate change movement. Foster believes strongly in the power of young activists. He has inspired many other young people to follow his example!

Jerome Foster II

EARLY START

Foster was concerned about climate change from an early age. His parents encouraged him to do something. In 2017, Foster created a virtual reality company that helped people see the world from others' perspectives. He also started *The Climate Reporter*. This news website is dedicated to sharing stories about environmental issues.

A SEAT AT THE TABLE

In 2019, Foster began an internship with U.S. congressman John Lewis. He learned about how climate change issues related to other **social justice** concerns. The same year, he cofounded Waic Up, an organization empowering young people to advocate for social, climate, and economic justice.

TIMELINE

2017
launches *The Climate Reporter*

2019
begins weekly climate strikes

WHITE HOUSE HELPER

People were impressed by Foster's activism. In 2021, he was invited to join a council to advise the White House on environmental issues. The council works to find fair solutions to fight climate change.

ALWAYS AN ACTIVIST

Foster has never stopped fighting for the climate. In 2024, he began working with American Forests to help protect trees across the U.S. He fights for other issues, too. His OneMillionOfUs organization helps young voters.

WASHINGTON, D.C.

AWARDS AND HONORS

- **2018** D.C. State Board of Education Leadership and Commitment Award
- **2019** Union of Concerned Scientists Defender of Science Award
- **2022** Captain Planet Foundation Young Superhero for Earth Award

BORN: May 9, 2002, in Washington, D.C.

EDUCATION: Pace University

KNOWN FOR: started the Waic Up organization to inspire youth to take action on climate change

FEBRUARY 2019 begins interning for congressman John Lewis

JULY 2019 cofounds Waic Up

2021 becomes a White House advisor on climate change

CIVIL RIGHTS ACTIVISTS

Dr. Martin Luther King Jr. was a leader of the civil rights movement. He organized and led peaceful protests that helped improve the rights of Black Americans and end **segregation**.

"Injustice anywhere is a threat to justice everywhere."
—Dr. Martin Luther King Jr., "Letter from Birmingham Jail"

Martin Luther King Jr.

ATLANTA

BORN: January 15, 1929, in Atlanta, Georgia

DIED: April 4, 1968

EDUCATION: Morehouse College, Crozer Theological Seminary, Boston University

KNOWN FOR: civil rights leader who demanded equality for Black Americans

EARLY LIFE

King grew up in Georgia during a time of segregation. As a teenager, he traveled north to work on a farm. He was inspired by how Black and white people ate at the same restaurants and attended the same churches.

CIVIL RIGHTS LEADER

King eventually settled in Montgomery, Alabama. He worked as a pastor in a church. In 1955, Rosa Parks was arrested for refusing to give up her bus seat to a white man. King helped organize a boycott of Montgomery's bus system. After a year, the boycott was successful. Black people could now sit anywhere on buses.

MARCHING FOR FREEDOM

King continued to work for equality. He became well-known nationwide. On August 28, 1963, he led the March on Washington for Jobs and Freedom. The purpose was to demand voting rights, education, and an end to segregation. King delivered his famous "I Have a Dream" speech to over 250,000 people.

DREAMING ON

King was arrested and threatened, but he never gave up. In 1968, he was killed in Tennessee. But he continues to inspire civil rights leaders. Americans honor King every year on Martin Luther King Jr. Day.

AWARDS AND HONORS

- **1957** Spingarn Medal
- **1964** Nobel Peace Prize
- **1977** Presidential Medal of Freedom

TIMELINE

1955 helps organize the Montgomery Bus Boycott

APRIL 1963 writes his famous "Letter from Birmingham Jail" after being arrested for protesting

AUGUST 1963 leads the March on Washington for Jobs and Freedom

1965 marches from Selma to Montgomery to demand fair voting rights

1968 leads the Poor People's Campaign in a march on Washington

TIMELINE

1970
speaks before the U.S. Senate in support of the Equal Rights Amendment

1971
helps start the National Women's Political Caucus

DECEMBER 1971
starts *Ms.* magazine

1993
is added to the National Women's Hall of Fame

2016
hosts the TV series *Woman with Gloria Steinem*

Gloria Steinem

Gloria Steinem is a writer and **feminist** who became one of the most important leaders of the women's rights movement. Her many books, articles, and speeches have raised awareness about issues women face. Her work also helped get more women elected to public office.

A YOUNG WRITER

Steinem went to college to study government. She graduated in 1956 and within a few years found work as a newspaper and magazine writer. Steinem wanted to write about politics. But her editors did not think women could write about serious subjects. In 1968, Steinem cofounded *New York* magazine. Now, she could write about anything she wanted.

BECOMING AN ACTIVIST

In the late 1960s, Steinem became interested in feminism. She became a spokesperson for the feminist movement, fighting for **reproductive** rights and other issues.

MOVING INTO POLITICS

Steinem was also a supporter of the Equal Rights Amendment (ERA). This would guarantee equal treatment regardless of gender. In 1970, Steinem spoke before the U.S. Senate in support of the ERA. But the amendment did not pass.

EARLY TRAVELER

As a child, Steinem and her parents traveled the country in a travel trailer. She did not start attending school regularly until she was 11!

FEMINIST ICON

In 1971, Steinem helped start the National Women's Political Caucus. It helps women get more involved in government. Today, Steinem remains a symbol of the feminist movement.

BORN: March 25, 1934, in Toledo, Ohio

EDUCATION: Smith College

KNOWN FOR: founded many organizations centered on women's rights

AWARDS AND HONORS

- **2012** American Humanist Association Humanist of the Year
- **2013** Presidential Medal of Freedom
- **2014** New York Women's Foundation Century Award

Phyllis Schlafly was a famous writer and **conservative** activist. One of her best-known accomplishments was a campaign to prevent the ERA from passing in the 1970s.

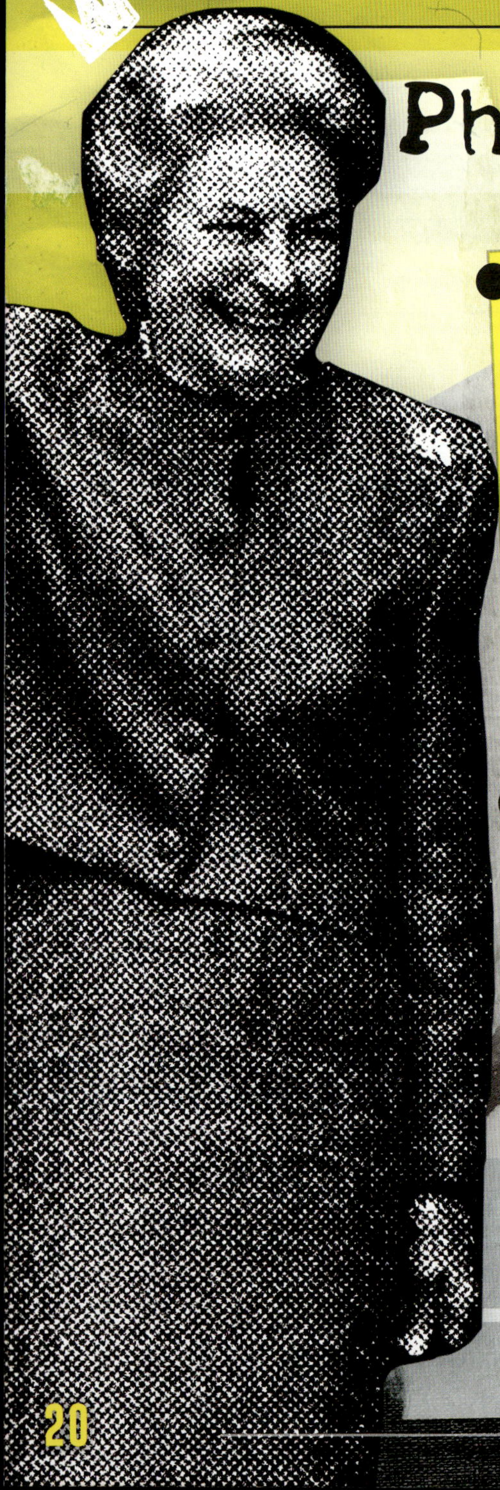

Phyllis Schlafly

EARLY WORK

Schlafly graduated from Washington University in 1944. The following year, she earned a master's degree in government from Radcliffe College. She worked on political campaigns and as a research librarian. In 1949, she got married. She left paid work to raise six children. But she remained active in politics. In 1964, Schlafly published her first book. It sold more than 3 million copies!

STOP ERA

In the 1970s, Schlafly launched a campaign to stop the ERA. The amendment would guarantee women equal rights to men. Schlafly feared that under the law, women would lose immunity from military service and legal benefits given to mothers and wives. Her STOP ERA movement grew to more than 20,000 members. Because of the group's work, the ERA did not become law.

TIMELINE

1945 earns a master's degree in government from Radcliffe College

1952 runs for the U.S. House of Representatives

A LEGENDARY LADY

Schlafly remained a conservative activist for the rest of her life. She influenced many presidents. She also published a newsletter and more than 20 books supporting her ideas about feminism and other issues.

BORN: August 15, 1924, in St. Louis, Missouri

DIED: September 5, 2016

EDUCATION: Washington University, Radcliffe College

KNOWN FOR: started the STOP ERA movement

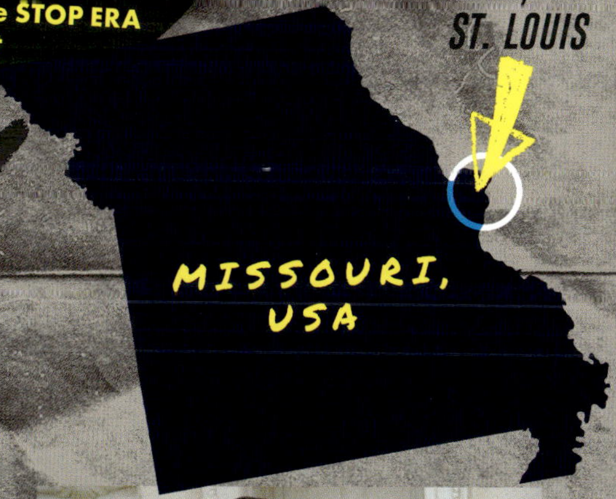

AWARDS AND HONORS

- **2008** Washington University Honorary Doctor of Humane Letters
- **2009** Clare Boothe Luce Policy Institute Lifetime Achievement Award
- **2010** Defender of Life Award

1964 publishes her first book, *A Choice Not an Echo*

1972 speaks out against the ERA in her newsletter, leading to the STOP ERA movement

1978 earns a law degree from Washington University

Judy Heumann

Judy Heumann was an activist who fought for people with disabilities. Her work led to many improvements for disabled people in the U.S.

A FIGHT FOR EDUCATION

When Heumann was a child, she became sick with **polio**. As a result, she needed a wheelchair. But her local school would not allow wheelchair users in classrooms. Her parents had to fight for her to attend school.

CAMP COUNSELOR

Heumann worked as a counselor at a camp for children with disabilities. In 2020, the camp and Heumann were featured in the documentary film *Crip Camp: A Disability Revolution.*

BORN: December 18, 1947, in Philadelphia, Pennsylvania

DIED: March 4, 2023

EDUCATION: Long Island University; University of California, Berkeley

KNOWN FOR: founded Disabled in Action and led the 504 Sit-in

THE FIGHT CONTINUES

As an adult, Heumann decided to become a teacher. She finished college in 1969. But she was denied a teaching license because of her wheelchair. Heumann filed a **lawsuit** to fight the decision. She won!

DISABLED IN ACTION

Heumann soon left teaching to focus on fighting for the rights of disabled people. In 1970, Heumann cofounded Disabled in Action (DIA). The organization fought for equal rights for people with disabilities.

THE 504 SIT-IN

In 1973, Heumann worked to help pass a law to protect disabled people from **discrimination**. In 1977, she led a sit-in when government leaders refused to honor a part of the law called Section 504. This pressured the government to enforce the law. It paved the way for the 1990 Americans with Disabilities Act (ADA).

LATER LIFE

Heumann continued her activism for the rest of her life. She advised U.S. presidents and gave speeches around the world.

AWARDS AND HONORS

- **2017** InterAction Lifetime Achievement Award
- **2018** National Council on Independent Living Women's Caucus Award
- **2022** Women's Entrepreneurship Day Organization Humanitarian Pioneer Award

TIMELINE

- **1970** cofounds Disabled in Action
- **1973** works to help pass the Rehabilitation Act of 1973
- **1977** leads the 504 Sit-in
- **1993** is appointed Assistant Secretary for the Office of Special Education and Rehabilitation Services
- **2020** publishes her memoir, *Being Heumann: An Unrepentant Memoir of a Disability Rights Activist*

Stacey Abrams

TIMELINE

2006 is elected to the Georgia House of Representatives

2013 founds the New Georgia Project

2018 loses election for governor of Georgia and founds Fair Fight Action

2021 is nominated for the Nobel Peace Prize

2022 runs for governor of Georgia and loses

Stacey Abrams is a U.S. politician and civil rights activist. In 2018, she made history for being the first Black woman nominated by a major political party to run for governor. But Abrams is best known for her fight for voter rights.

A YOUNG ACTIVIST

Abrams spent most of her childhood in Gulfport, Mississippi. Her parents encouraged her to fight for what she believed in. In college, she began organizing and attending civil rights protests. She went on to become a lawyer.

IN THE HOUSE

In 2006, Abrams was elected to the Georgia House of Representatives. She worked toward better health care and **criminal justice** reform. In 2013, she founded the New Georgia Project. It helped register 86,000 new voters!

MOVING INTO POLITICS

In 2018, Abrams ran to become Georgia's governor. The election was close, but Abrams lost. Many people were removed from the voter lists before the election. People believed this was done on purpose. Abrams founded Fair Fight Action to fight **voter suppression**. The organization has helped register more than 800,000 voters in Georgia.

MORE WORK

Abrams has written several books and given speeches around the world. In 2022, she ran for governor again. She lost, but she continues to be an important voice for voter rights.

> "Progress is possible, but it is fragile - and across our country, the battles for our most basic civil rights rage on."
> — Stacey Abrams

BORN: December 9, 1973, in Madison, Wisconsin

EDUCATION: Spelman College, Lyndon B. Johnson School of Public Affairs at the University of Texas at Austin, Yale Law School

KNOWN FOR: founded the New Georgia Project and Fair Fight Action

AWARDS AND HONORS

- **2012** John F. Kennedy New Frontier Award
- **2014** Gabrielle Giffords Rising Star Award
- **2019** University of Texas LBJ School of Public Affairs Distinguished Public Servant Award

HUMAN RIGHTS ACTIVISTS

When Malala Yousafzai was a child, her school was shut down by a group that did not want girls to get an education. Yousafzai spoke out against them. Her fight for human rights made her famous around the world.

Malala Yousafzai

A DESIRE TO LEARN

When Yousafzai was 10, new leaders in Pakistan made it illegal for girls to go to school. They closed and even destroyed many girls' schools. Girls faced violence for disobeying. But Yousafzai did not step down. She began writing articles about life under the new rules. In 2009, she appeared on TV to protest the rules. She became well known for speaking out. This made her a target to her region's new rulers. In 2012, she was attacked for speaking out.

SURVIVOR

Yousafzai survived and continued to speak out. After recovering, she gave a speech in front of the UN in 2013. She stood up for girls' right to education. The same year, she published a book about her life. She also started the Malala Fund to help provide free and safe education for girls around the world.

MORE ACTIVISM

Yousafzai became the youngest person to earn a Nobel Peace Prize in 2014. The next year, she opened a school for **refugee** girls in Lebanon. Her work continues to help people around the world.

AWARDS AND HONORS

- **2011** International Children's Peace Prize nominee
- **2014** Nobel Peace Prize
- **2017** UN Messenger of Peace

BORN: July 12, 1997, in Mingora, Pakistan

EDUCATION: University of Oxford

KNOWN FOR: fights for girls' right to education

"I truly believe the only way we can create global peace is through not only educating our minds, but our hearts and our souls."
—Malala Yousafzai

TIMELINE

- **2008** gives her first public speech
- **2012** survives an attack after speaking out for her beliefs
- **2013** gives a famous speech before the UN
- **2015** opens a school for refugee girls in Lebanon
- **2020** graduates from the University of Oxford

Dolores Huerta

Dolores Huerta is a famous labor rights activist. Her efforts have improved conditions for farmworkers across the U.S.

GIVING BACK

Huerta spent her early years in Stockton, California, where many immigrant farmworkers lived. When she grew up and became a teacher, Huerta taught the children of many of these workers. The children often came to school hungry. Their families had little money. Huerta left teaching to help the workers fight for better treatment.

A NEW UNION

In 1955, Huerta helped start a branch of the Community Service Organization (CSO). It worked to improve the lives of Latino people in the community. While at CSO, Huerta cofounded the National Farm Workers Association (NFWA) in 1962. This union fought for better working conditions.

DELANO GRAPE STRIKE

In 1965, Huerta led a strike of 5,000 grape farmworkers in Delano, California. The strikers demanded better pay and safer working conditions. The farm owners hired replacement workers. But the strikers did not give up. They boycotted stores that sold products made from the farms' grapes. After five years, the farm owners agreed to the workers' demands.

YES WE CAN!

Huerta was the first to use the Spanish phrase "¡Sí Se Puede!" as a slogan. In 2008, Barack Obama used an English version of this phrase, "Yes we can!" as his campaign slogan.

TIMELINE

- **1955** helps start the Stockton chapter of the CSO
- **1962** cofounds the NFWA

BORN: April 10, 1930, in Dawson, New Mexico

EDUCATION: Stockton College

KNOWN FOR: led important strikes and boycotts and cofounded the NFWA

NEVER GIVE UP

In 1973, Huerta led a consumer grape boycott. This led to California's Agricultural Labor Relations Act of 1975. This law let farmworkers form unions and demand better pay. Huerta continued to fight for workers' rights and worked to get more women and Latino people elected.

AWARDS AND HONORS

- **1993** National Women's Hall of Fame
- **1999** Eleanor Roosevelt Human Rights Award
- **2012** Presidential Medal of Freedom

1965 leads a successful strike of 5,000 farmworkers

2003 starts the Dolores Huerta Foundation

2017 the film *Dolores* is released, exploring Huerta's life and activism

When David Hogg was a teenager, he survived a shooting at his high school. He was angry at lawmakers for not doing more to protect students. Today, he is one of the best-known gun control activists.

David Hogg

A LIFE-CHANGING EXPERIENCE

In 2018, Hogg was a student at Marjory Stoneman Douglas High School in Parkland, Florida. That year, a gunman entered the school. The attacker killed 17 students and staff members and injured another 17. Hogg recorded interviews with his classmates as they hid from the attacker. His videos quickly gained attention from the media.

MARCH FOR OUR LIVES

Right after the attack, Hogg began giving interviews about his experience. He used these appearances to argue for stronger gun control laws. Hogg joined with other students to organize a protest in Washington, D.C. On March 24, 2018, around 800,000 protestors joined the event, called March for Our Lives. Hogg gave a passionate speech in front of the crowd. It was viewed by people around the world. The March for Our Lives organization continues to push for stricter gun control laws.

BESTSELLER ★

Hogg's sister Lauren also survived the Parkland attack. In 2018, Hogg and his sister published the bestselling book *#NeverAgain* about their experiences.

ENCOURAGING YOUNG LEADERS

Hogg continued his activism after the march. In 2023, he launched an organization called Leaders We Deserve. It works to get more young people elected as politicians.

BORN: April 12, 2000, in Los Angeles, California

EDUCATION: Marjory Stoneman Douglas High School, Harvard University

KNOWN FOR: cofounded March for Our Lives and Leaders We Deserve

AWARDS AND HONORS

- **2018** International Children's Peace Prize
- **2019** PRWeek U.S. Communicator of the Year
- **2022** Mahatma Gandhi Center for Global Nonviolence National Nonviolence Award

TIMELINE

- **FEBRUARY 2018** survives the shooting at Marjory Stoneman Douglas High School
- **MARCH 2018** helps organize and lead March for Our Lives in Washington, D.C.
- **JUNE 2018** *#NeverAgain* is published
- **2019** begins attending college at Harvard University
- **2023** launches Leaders We Deserve

George Takei

George Takei became famous as an actor in the TV show *Star Trek*. But he used his fame to bring attention to important human rights issues. He is an advocate for **LGBTQ+** rights, including same-sex marriage.

A CHILDHOOD BEHIND BARS

Takei's family is Japanese American. When Takei was young, he and his family were forced to move to an **internment camp** along with other people with Japanese backgrounds. They spent around three years in the camp. They lost their home, money, and business. The camps had poor living conditions. Takei never forgot the way his family was treated.

BECOMING AN ACTIVIST

In 1966, Takei began playing Hikaru Sulu on *Star Trek*. The role made him famous. He used his fame to draw attention to human rights issues. He demanded the U.S. government to apologize for its treatment of Japanese Americans. He also protested the Vietnam War. In the 1990s, President Bill Clinton appointed Takei to the Japan-U.S. Friendship Commission.

AWARDS AND HONORS

- **2004** Order of the Rising Sun, Gold Rays with Rosette
- **2014** GLAAD Vito Russo Award
- **2015** Japanese American National Museum Distinguished Medal of Honor for Lifetime Achievement and Public Service

ONE OF MANY

From 1942 to 1946, around 120,000 Japanese Americans were imprisoned in 10 internment camps across the U.S.

TIMELINE

- **1942** is forced to leave home for an internment camp
- **1966** becomes an actor on *Star Trek*

BORN: April 20, 1937, in Los Angeles, California

EDUCATION: University of California, Los Angeles

KNOWN FOR: drew attention to U.S. internment camps and fights for LGBTQ+ rights

LGBTQ+ ACTIVISM

In 2005, the California governor refused to sign a bill that would make same-sex marriage legal. Takei believed that same-sex couples should have the same rights as everyone else. He announced that he was gay and became a prominent LGBTQ+ activist. Takei continues to use his fame to draw attention to LGBTQ+ and other human rights issues. Much of his activism takes place on social media, where he has millions of followers.

2005 comes out as gay

2016 founds One Pulse for America to fight gun violence

2019 co-writes the graphic novel *They Called Us Enemy,* based on his experiences in internment camps

Bryan Stevenson is a lawyer known for his work helping people in prison. His work has helped free more than 100 people who were wrongly convicted. It has also led to new laws to protect the rights of Americans.

Bryan Stevenson

A STIRRING EXPERIENCE

Stevenson grew up with his family in Delaware. When Stevenson was 16, his grandfather was killed by a group of teenagers. They were sentenced to life in prison. Stevenson loved his grandfather. But he also questioned if the teenagers deserved a life sentence. He began thinking more about criminal justice. He went on to earn a law degree from Harvard University in 1985.

EQUAL JUSTICE INITIATIVE

Stevenson knew poor people and people of color were treated differently by courts. He began working to help people in prison. In 1989, he founded the Equal Justice Initiative (EJI). It helps prisoners who cannot afford to pay for lawyers. It has helped **exonerate** people falsely convicted. It has also helped shorten sentences for people convicted as minors.

AWARDS AND HONORS

- **1991** ACLU National Medal of Liberty
- **2000** Olaf Palme Prize
- **2004** National Lawyers Guild Lawyer for the People Award
- **2016** Thurgood Marshall Award

CHANGING THE LAW

With EJI, Stevenson has worked to change laws to protect people in prison. In 2012, he won a Supreme Court ruling that determined mandatory sentences of life without **parole** for minors were unconstitutional. In 2019, he won a ruling that protected people with **dementia** from **capital punishment**. His work has helped make criminal justice in the U.S. more fair.

BORN: November 14, 1959, in Milton, Delaware

EDUCATION: Eastern University, Harvard University

KNOWN FOR: founded the EJI and works to help people in prison

JUST MERCY

Stevenson released *Just Mercy: A Story of Justice and Redemption* in 2014. This book follows Stevenson's work to help wrongfully convicted people.

TIMELINE

1985 earns a law degree from Harvard University

1989 founds the EJI

1998 becomes a law professor at New York University

2012 wins a Supreme Court ruling banning minors from being sentenced to life without parole

2019 wins a Supreme Court ruling protecting prisoners with dementia from capital punishment

Ayọ Tometi

In 2013, Ayọ Tometi cofounded the Black Lives Matter (BLM) movement with two friends. She has since become a powerful activist for social justice and human rights causes.

EARLY ACTIVISM

Tometi grew up in Arizona, where her parents were **undocumented** Nigerian immigrants. She watched as they and other immigrants in their community faced threats of **deportation**. This inspired Tometi to work on the U.S. border with Mexico to make sure incoming people were treated fairly. After finishing college, she got a job with an organization that supported the rights of Black immigrants.

BLACK LIVES MATTER

In 2013, Tometi cofounded BLM in response to the **acquittal** of a man charged with killing a Black teenager. This movement drew attention to the inequality Black Americans experience, especially from law enforcement. More police killings of Black people led to more BLM protests worldwide. Millions of people demanded fair treatment of Black people by the police.

IN A NAME

Tometi's birth name was Opal Tometi. On October 1, 2021, she changed her name to Ayọ to honor her Nigerian background.

TIMELINE

2005 graduates from the University of Arizona

2011 begins working with the Black Alliance for Just Immigration

AWARDS AND HONORS

- **2015** National Black Caucus of State Legislators Humanitarian Award
- **2017** Letelier-Moffitt Human Rights Award
- **2019** Coretta Scott King Center Legacy Award

BORN: August 15, 1984, in Phoenix, Arizona

EDUCATION: University of Arizona, Arizona State University

KNOWN FOR: cofounded the BLM movement

HER WORK CONTINUES

In 2020, Tometi founded Diaspora Rising, an organization dedicated to connecting Black people around the world. In 2021, she joined the International Living Future Institute. It works to help people connect with the natural world. For Tometi, the fight for people to live safe, healthy lives is only beginning.

- **2013** cofounds Black Lives Matter
- **2020** founds Diaspora Rising
- **2021** joins the International Living Future Institute

ANIMAL RIGHTS ACTIVISTS

Temple Grandin is an animal scientist and professor. Her work has helped people understand animals better. Her designs have helped reduce fear and stress in farm animals.

Temple Grandin

A LOVE OF ANIMALS

From a young age, Grandin had trouble communicating. She later found out that she has autism. She went to a private high school. There, she discovered a love of horses. This grew into an interest in how animals think and feel. She believed that her autism helped her understand animals better than most people.

HELPING FARM ANIMALS

Grandin studied psychology in college before earning her doctorate in animal science. Meanwhile, she worked in the cattle industry. She noticed the animals reacted poorly to different machines. She invented a new system that would help livestock stay calm in stressful situations. Today, half of U.S. cattle farms use equipment Grandin designed.

TWO SIDES

Many support Grandin's work in helping livestock stay calm. Others do not approve. They believe that raising livestock to be eaten is wrong.

OTHER WORK

Grandin's work also includes books and speeches about autism. In 1995, she published *Thinking in Pictures*. The book explores how her mind works as a person with autism. In 2005, she published the bestseller *Animals in Translation*. The book explores animal behavior through autism. In 2010, Grandin gave a talk about the different kinds of minds and how they can work together. Millions of people watched it!

AWARDS AND HONORS

2015 World Organization for Animal Health Meritorious Award

2017 National Women's Hall of Fame

2024 Animal Welfare Institute Schweitzer Medal

BORN: August 29, 1947, in Boston, Massachusetts

EDUCATION: Franklin Pierce College, Arizona State University, University of Illinois at Urbana-Champaign

KNOWN FOR: invented a widely used system to calm livestock

TIMELINE

1970s invents system to calm livestock

1990 begins teaching at Colorado State University

1995 publishes *Thinking in Pictures*

2005 publishes the bestseller *Animals in Translation*

2010 gives a viral talk about her experiences with autism, which is viewed more than 7 million times

Jane Goodall

Jane Goodall spent many years working with chimpanzees in Tanzania. She discovered they were much more intelligent than people realized. She dedicated her life to protecting the animals. Goodall's work has changed how people think about animals and **conservation**.

AFRICAN DREAMS

From a young age, Goodall loved animals. She dreamed of traveling to Africa to study animals. In her early 20s, she traveled to Kenya. There, she began working for scientist Dr. Louis Leakey. In 1960, he sent her to Tanzania to study chimpanzees. Goodall was the first person to discover they use tools. She observed how they interacted with one another. She even watched the first-ever documented war between chimpanzees.

TIMELINE

1957 travels to Kenya and begins working for Dr. Louis Leakey

1960 begins studying chimpanzees in Tanzania

1965 earns a doctorate in ethology from the University of Cambridge

1977 founds the Jane Goodall Institute

2020 launches a podcast called *The Jane Goodall Hopecast*

AWARDS AND HONORS

- **2002** UN Messenger of Peace
- **2021** Templeton Prize
- **2022** Stephen Hawking Medal for Science Communication

ANIMAL ACTIVISM

In time, Goodall began to focus more on conservation. She realized that chimpanzees were in danger from habitat loss. In 1977, she founded the Jane Goodall Institute. It supports chimpanzee research and conservation. In 1991, Goodall cofounded Roots & Shoots. It works with people around the world to turn young people into conservationists.

LATER LIFE

Goodall continued to travel the world speaking about animal conservation. She wrote several books and papers about these subjects. In 2020, she launched a podcast to help her connect with audiences around the world. Goodall has never stopped fighting for her beloved chimpanzees.

> "What you do makes a difference, and you have to decide what kind of difference you want to make."
> —Jane Goodall

BORN: April 3, 1934, in London, England

EDUCATION: University of Cambridge

KNOWN FOR: studied chimpanzees and promoted conservation through the Jane Goodall Institute

Paula Kahumbu is an **ecologist** and conservationist who works to protect elephants and other African wildlife. She believes storytelling is the secret to conservation.

Paula Kahumbu

A LOVE OF ELEPHANTS

As a child, Kahumbu lived in Nairobi, Kenya, near conservationist Richard Leakey. He taught her about the animals in their area. Kahumbu decided to turn her love of animals into a career. In the 1980s, she helped study tusks the Kenyan government had taken back from **poachers**. She became interested in elephant conservation. She earned her doctorate in 2002 after studying elephants on Kenya's coast. She decided to do whatever she could to protect elephants and other wildlife.

A NEW ROLE

In 2007, Kahumbu became the leader of WildlifeDirect, an organization that supports wildlife conservation. Under Kahumbu's leadership, Hands Off Our Elephants began in 2013. This project works to prevent elephant poaching. In 2018, Kahumbu helped launch Wildlife Warriors Kids under WildlifeDirect. It teaches Kenyan children about science.

TIMELINE

2007 becomes the leader of WildlifeDirect

2013 starts Hands Off Our Elephants

ACTIVISM THROUGH STORIES

In 2019, Kahumbu began hosting *Wildlife Warriors.* This TV series introduces children to Kenyan people who protect wildlife. In 2023, Kahumbu hosted a four-part National Geographic documentary called *Secrets of the Elephants.* Her work inspires people to protect animals.

AWARDS AND HONORS

- **2015** Order of the Grand Warrior Award
- **2021** Whitley Gold Award
- **2021** Rolex National Geographic Explorer of the Year

HIPPO HELPER

In 2004, Kahumbu helped rescue a baby hippopotamus. She helped it find safety in a sanctuary, where it befriended a tortoise. She eventually co-wrote a children's book about the duo!

BORN: June 25, 1966, in Nairobi, Kenya

EDUCATION: University of Bristol, University of Florida Gainesville, Princeton University, University of Pretoria

KNOWN FOR: works to protect elephants and promote animal conservation

- **2018** helps launch Wildlife Warriors Kids
- **2019** begins hosting *Wildlife Warriors*
- **2023** National Geographic releases *Secrets of the Elephants*

THE FUTURE OF ACTIVISM

From conservationists to social justice advocates, activists are fighting to make the world a better place. New issues emerge every day that need attention. Luckily, a new generation of young activists is ready to rise to the challenge!

MORE ACTIVISTS TODAY AND BEYOND

XIUHTEZCATL MARTINEZ

Xiuhtezcatl Martinez is a hip-hop artist who uses his art to bring attention to environmental issues. He worked with Earth Guardians to encourage other young people to make a difference by helping the environment.

LESEIN MUTUNKEI

At age 12, Lesein Mutunkei founded Trees4Goals to fight deforestation in his native Kenya. He decided to plant trees every time he scored a goal while playing soccer. By 2022, Trees4Goals had planted more than 5,000 trees.

MARI COPENY

Mari Copeny grew up in Flint, Michigan, where the water was unsafe to drink. At age 8, she wrote a letter to President Obama asking for help. Since then, she has raised money and supplies to help people in her community get clean water and live better lives.

THANDIWE CHAMA

Thandiwe Chama was 8 years old when her school closed down because it did not have enough teachers. There was an AIDS epidemic in Zambia where she lived. She decided to fight to ensure that every child has access to education. She also raises awareness about AIDS treatment and prevention.

MARLEY DIAS

Marley Dias was frustrated when most of the books assigned to her in school featured white, male characters. She founded #1000BlackGirlBooks to collect books featuring Black female characters to donate to schools.

GENESIS BUTLER

Genesis Butler raises money for rescued farm animals and has spoken out against the meat industry's treatment of animals. She also draws attention to how factory farming worsens climate change.

GLOSSARY

acquittal—a judgment that a person is not guilty of a crime

AIDS—a disease that makes a person's immune system weak and can cause illnesses to become deadly; AIDS stands for acquired immunodeficiency syndrome.

apartheid—a policy that separated and discriminated against people based on their race

capital punishment—the practice of killing people as punishment for serious crimes

climate change—a human-caused change in Earth's weather due to warming temperatures

conservation—the careful protection of something

conservative—supporting existing views, ways of life, or institutions

criminal justice—related to the system that determines penalties for people who have committed crimes

dementia—one of a group of brain disorders that impacts memory and behavior

deportation—the act of forcing someone to leave a country

discrimination—the act of treating someone unfairly because of race, gender, age, or other differences

ecologist—a scientist who studies the natural world

exonerate—to clear someone of a crime after they have been convicted of it

feminist—a person who believes that people of all genders should have equal rights and opportunities

Indigenous—related to people originally from an area

internment camp—a prison camp people may be forced into during times of war; people in internment camps are not convicted of crimes.

lawsuit—a disagreement between two people or groups that is brought before a court

LGBTQ+—a community of people who identify as something other than heterosexual or the gender they were assigned at birth; LGBTQ+ stands for lesbian, gay, transgender, queer, and other identities.

parole—the release of a prisoner before their sentence is over

pesticides—chemicals used to control the growth of weeds or insects

petition—a written call to action signed by many different people

poachers—people who illegally hunt animals

polio—a disease that affects the nervous system and can make a person unable to move parts of their body

refugee—a person who flees their home for safety

reproductive—related to the act of becoming pregnant or giving birth

social justice—the idea that people from all backgrounds deserve equal rights

segregation—the practice of separating people based on their race

undocumented—not having legal paperwork that shows the right to be in a place

voter suppression—the act of intentionally preventing people from voting

WRITE ABOUT IT!

- Is there a cause you believe enough to be an activist for? **What is it and why?**

- Are there any activists in this book that you strongly agree or disagree with? **Why?**

- Are there any examples of activism in your community? **What are they?**

ALSO CHECK OUT

INDEX

The images in this book are reproduced through the courtesy of: Marion S. Trikosko/ Wikimedia Commons, front cover (King Jr.), p. 3 (King); Adam Chitayat/ Wikimedia Commons, front cover (Yousafazai), pp. 3 (Yousafzai), 26 (Yousafzai); East Asia and Pacific Media Hub U.S. Department of State/ Wikimedia Commons, front cover (Heumann), pp. 22 (Heumann large), 27 (Yousafzai top photo); Birdie Thompson/ AdMedia/ Alamy Stock Photo, p. 3 (Takei); Erik McGregor/ Getty Images, pp. 4-5 (main); XcepticZP/ Wikimedia Commons, p. 5 (1945); Ebony Magazine/ Wikimedia Commons, p. 5 (1955-1956); David Keep, p. 5 (1973); Rena Schild, p. 5 (2015); COP21/ Alamy Stock Photo, p. 5 (2015 Paris Agreement); roberjzm, p. 6 (environmental activism); Rawpixel.com, p. 6 (animal rights activism); Library of the London School of Economics and Political Science/ Wikimedia Commons, p. 7 (Mandela); or Balkowitsch/ Wikimedia Commons, p. 7 (LaDuke); Jon Tadiello/ Wikimedia Commons, p. 7 (Burke); Elliott & Fry/ Wikimedia Commons, p. 7 (Gandhi); Kushal Das/ Wikimedia Commons, p. 8 (Thunberg large); Streetsblog Denver/ Wikimedia Commons, p. 8 (Thunberg small top); Leonhard Lenz/ Wikimedia Commons, p. 8 (Thunberg bottom); Stefan Müller/ Wikimedia Commons, p. 9 (Thunberg profile); JohnNilsson, p. 9 (Stockholm); Liv Oeian, p. 9 (superpower); Shawn Goldberg/ SOPA Images/ Sipa USA/ Alamy Stock Photo, p. 10 (Autumn Peltier large); Vaughn Ridley/ Collision via Sportsfile/ spacing.ca, p. 10 (Autumn Peltier small); David Niviere/ ABACAPRESS.COM/ Alamy Stock Photo, p. 11 (Peltier Warrior Up); Pernelle Voyage, p. 11 (Manitoulin Island, Ontario); Collision Conf/ flickr, p. 11 (Peltier profile); Laura A. Macaluso, Ph.D./ Wikimedia Commons, p. 12 (Carson Monument); Cv822/ Wikimedia Commons, p. 12 (Springdale); Theo's Little/ Wikimedia, p. 13 (book); Science History Images/ Alamy Stock Photo, p. 13 (Carson profile); Smithsonian Institution/ Wikimedia Commons, p. 13 (Carson large); Adeleloves4earth/ Wikimedia Commons, p. 14 (Foster II small); Billy Bennight/ ZUMA Press Wire/ Alamy Stock Photo, p. 14 (Foster II large); Mudrova Nikol, p. 14 (small bottom photo); Sergey Novikov, p. 15 (Washington, D.C.); Phil Pasquini, p. 15 (Foster II); Prince Williams/ Getty Images, p. 15 (Foster II profile); Rowland Scherman/ Adam Cuerden/ Wikimedia Commons, p. 16 (King Jr. top); Kevin Ruck, pp. 16 (Atlanta), 37 (Phoenix); Hugo van Gelderen/ Anefo/ Wikimedia Commons, p. 16 (King Jr. profile); Dick DeMarsico/ Wikimedia Commons, p. 16 (King Jr. large); National Park Service/ Wikimedia Commons, p. 17 (King Jr.); Liberty Media for Women, LLC/ Wikimedia Commons, p. 18 (*Ms.*); Gage Skidmore/ Wikimedia Commons, pp. 19 (Gloria Steinem small top), 20 (Schlafly small), 21 (Schlafly top right), 25 (Abrams profile), 28 (Huerta small top), 33 (Takei profile); Felix Mizioznikov, p. 19 (Toledo); Jay Godwin/ Wikimedia Commons, pp. 19 (Steinem profile), 35 (Stevenson profile); Lynn Gilbert/ Wikimedia Commons, p. 19 (Steinem large); Mark Taylor/ Wikimedia Commons, p. 20 (Schlafly large); GrahamHardy/ Wikimedia Commons, p. 20 (book); Warren K. Leffler/ Wikimedia Commons, p. 21 (Schlafly profile); f11photo, pp. 21 (St. Louis), 22 (Philadelphia); White House Photographic Collection/ Wikimedia Commons, p. 21 (Schlafly bottom right); Senado Federal/ Wikimedia Commons, p. 22 (Heumann top); Evelyn Straus/ NY Daily News/ Getty Images, p. 22 (Heumann profile); Bailey Hill/ Wikimedia Commons, p. 23 (Heumann); LBJ School/ Wikimedia Commons, p. 24 (Abrams); James, p. 25 (Madison); Media Punch/ Alamy Stock Photo, pp. 25 (Abrams large), 30 (Hogg); Southbank Centre/ Wikimedia Commons, p. 27 (Yousafzai profile); hamdi bendali, p. 27 (book); SakhanPhotography, p. 27 (Mingora); Susan Ruggles/ Wikimedia Commons, p. 28 (Huerta); Everett Collection/ Alamy Stock Photo, p. 29 (Huerta large); Rafa213/ Wikimedia Commons, p. 29 (Huerta profile); Legends of America Archives/ Wikimedia Commons, p. 29 (Dawson); SOPA Images/ Alamy Stock Photo, p. 30 (bestseller); The White House/ Wikimedia Commons, p. 31 (Hoff profile); Newport Coast Media, p. 31 (Los Angeles); Lorie Shaull/ Wikimedia Commons, p. 31 (bottom photo); PARAMOUNT TELEVISION/ Alamy Stock Photo, p. 32 (top photo); Library of Congress Life/ Wikimedia Commons, p. 32 (middle photo); Trevor Cokley/ Wikimedia Commons, p. 32 (bottom photo); Birdie Thompson/ AdMedia/ Alamy Stock Photo, p. 33 (Takei large); SeanPavonePhoto, pp. 33 (Los Angeles), 39 (Boston); Stephen Smith/ SIPA USA/ Alamy Stock Photo, p. 34 (Stevenson); Khairil, p. 35 (Milton); U.S. Embassy The Hague/ Wikimedia Commons, p. 35 (Stevenson); Bryan Stevenson/ Wikimedia Commons, p. 35 (book); Web Summit Rio/ Wikimedia Commons, p. 36; Web Summit/ Wikimedia Commons, p. 37 (Tometi large, Tometi profile); Nancy Kaszerman/ ZUMA Press/ Alamy Stock Photo, p. 38 (top photo); Peabody Awards/ Alamy Stock Photo, p. 38 (Grandin large); Jonathunder/ Alamy Stock Photo, p. 39 (Temple Grandin profile); s4svisuals, p. 40 (London); U.S. Mission Uganda/ Wikimedia Commons, p. 40 (Goodall); Courtesy: CSU Archives/ Everett Collection/ Alamy Stock Photo, p. 41 (top photo); Kay & Karl Ammann/ Alamy Stock Photo, p. 41 (Goodall profile); U.S. Mission Uganda/ Alamy Stock Photo, p. 41 (Goodall large); Kris Krüg/ Wikimedia Commons, p. 42 (Kahumbu top small); Kengitau254/ Wikimedia Commons, p. 42 (Kahumbu large); USFWS Mountain-Prairie/ Wikimedia Commons, p. 43 (top right); Eric Isselée, p. 43 (hippo); eunikas, p. 43 (Nairobi); Gallo Images/ Beeld/ Wikus de Wet/ Getty Images, p. 43 (Kahumbu profile); wellphoto, p. 44 (microphone); Josué Rivas/ Wikimedia Commons, p. 44 (Martinez); ActionForNature/ ActionForNature Press Kit, p. 44 (Mutunkei); Jim Ruymen/ UPI/ Alamy Stock Photo, p. 45 (Copeny); Stephane Cardinale/ Getty Images, p. 45 (Chama); Anthony Behar/ Sipa USA/ Alamy Stock Photo, p. 45 (Dias); Nina Prommer/ Sipa USA/ Alamy Stock Photo, p. 45 (Butler).